Oregon Country: The History and Legacy of the Disputed Region & Treaty that Led to Oregon's Statehood

By Charles River Editors

1961 reenactment of pioneers along the Oregon Trail

About Charles River Editors

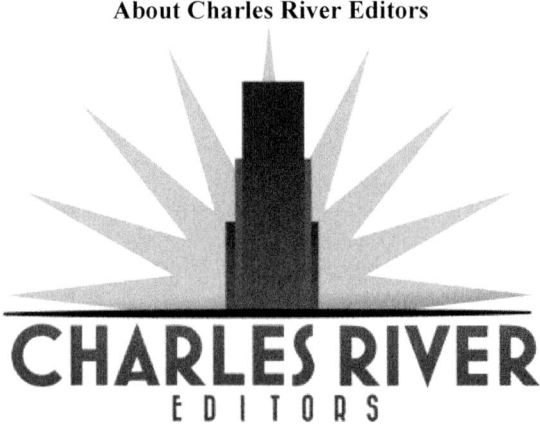

Charles River Editors is a boutique digital publishing company, specializing in bringing history back to life with educational and engaging books on a wide range of topics. Keep up to date with our new and free offerings with this 5 second sign up on our weekly mailing list, and visit Our Kindle Author Page to see other recently published Kindle titles.

We make these books for you and always want to know our readers' opinions, so we encourage you to leave reviews and look forward to publishing new and exciting titles each week.

Introduction

Alfred Jacob Miller's painting *Breaking up Camp at Sunrise*

The Oregon Country

The westward movement of Americans in the 19th century was one of the largest and most consequential migrations in history, and among the paths that blazed west, the most well-known is the Oregon Trail, which was not a single trail but a network of paths that began at one of four "jumping off" points. The eastern section of the Oregon Trail, which followed the Missouri River through Kansas, Nebraska, and Wyoming, was shared by people traveling along the California, Bozeman, and Mormon Trails. These trails branched off at various points, and the California Trail diverged from the Oregon Trail at Fort Hall in southern Idaho. From there, the Oregon Trail moved northward, along the Snake River, then through the Blue Mountains to Fort Walla Walla. From there, travelers would cross the prairie before reaching the Methodist mission at The Dalles, which roughly marked the end of the Trail.

The Trail stretched roughly half the country, and hundreds of thousands of settlers would use it, yet the Oregon Trail is famous not so much for its physical dimensions but for what it represented. As many who used the Oregon Trail described in memoirs, the West represented opportunities for adventure, independence, and fortune, and fittingly, the ever popular game named after the Oregon Trail captures that mentality and spirit by requiring players to safely move a party west to the end of the trail.

Perhaps most famously, the game that helped popularize current generations' interest in the Oregon Trail highlighted the obstacles the pioneers faced in moving West. Indeed, as all too many settlers discovered, traveling along the Trail was fraught with various kinds of obstacles and danger, including bitter weather, potentially deadly illnesses, and hostile Native Americans, not to mention an unforgiving landscape that famous American explorer Stephen Long deemed "unfit for human habitation." And while many would look back romantically at the Oregon Trail over time, 19th century Americans were all too happy and eager for the transcontinental railroad to help speed their passage west and render overland paths like the Oregon Trail obsolete.

Oregon Country: The History and Legacy of the Disputed Region and the Treaty that Led to Oregon's Statehood examines the land disputes, and how events unfolded on the way to Oregon becoming part of America. Along with pictures depicting important people, places, and events, you will learn about Oregon Country like never before.

Oregon Country: The History and Legacy of the Disputed Region and the Treaty that Led to Oregon's Statehood

About Charles River Editors

Introduction

   The Far Northwest

   American Exploration in the West

   Commercial Empires

   Increased Settlement

   The Oregon Treaty

   Statehood

   Online Resources

   Further Reading

Free Books by Charles River Editors

Discounted Books by Charles River Editors

The Far Northwest

"The fur of these animals, as mentioned in the Russian Accounts, is certainly softer and finer than others that we know of; and therefore the discovery of this part of the continent of North America, were so valuable an article of commerce may be met with, cannot be a matter of indifference." – Captain James Cook

In the first half of July 1776, two events took place that would radically transform the complexion of the known world. On July 4, the United States declared its independence from Britain while in the midst of the Revolution. A week later, on July 12, Captain James Cook set off from the Royal Navy Docks, Plymouth, commencing his third voyage of discovery. Commanding the HMS *Resolution* and leading the HMS *Discovery*, Cook would add the Pacific coast of North America to the growing British sphere of influence. His specific orders were to locate the Northwest Passage, which, in the late 18th century, was emerging as the Holy Grail of European navigation. Expeditions of this nature, however, tended to be opportunistic, and while the discovery of the Northwest Passage would have granted Cook a special place in the pantheon of naval explorers, it would offer little in the matter of strategic advantage. That lay in taking note of and observing regions of particular value to the British Empire.

Cook

Cook was by then arguably the captain with the most intimate knowledge of the Pacific Ocean. Over the course of two previous voyages, he had charted many of the far-flung islands, as well as the significant land-masses of Terra Australis and New Zealand. This time, rounding the Cape of Good Hope, Cook struck out across the southern Indian Ocean, revisiting Australia and New Zealand before arriving on the shores of the Pacific Northwest sometime in the spring of 1778. There, he encountered the kind of "vile, thick and stinking fogges" on the coast of Oregon that Sir Francis Drake experienced some two centuries earlier. On that voyage, Drake named the country, barely visible through the mist and rain, "Nova Albion," claiming it for Britain in a rather perfunctory ceremony before heading south back to the tropics and the lucrative business of robbing Spanish targets.

After Drake's brief visit and hasty departure, the Pacific Northwest remained unvisited, except perhaps for an occasional secretive Spanish expedition north from Mexico, until Cook arrived in 1778. The Spanish, of course, had a better sense of the northwest coast of America than any other European power, but they tended to keep their discoveries to themselves, so in general, the

British and French were unaware of much in the way of Spanish progress. These expeditions were, in any case, superficial, and no particular discoveries were made or documented.

Cook, on the other hand, took the same methodical approach as he had on his first two voyages, and his expedition of 1778 was recognized, for the most part, as the first modern, comprehensive mapping survey. It was certainly the first to help the Europeans actually understand the region. At the time, the parts of the coast indisputably claimed by Spain lay mainly below the 40th Parallel, and Cook was instructed not to approach the western seaboard at any point lower than that. Beyond that, he was ordered merely to proceed north along the coast to a latitude of 65 degrees, and if he found the Northwest Passage, he was to sail through it, remaining alert also for a Northeast Passage across the top of Russia. He was also to take detailed notes of possible natural resources and to take possession on behalf of the Crown any territory not claimed either by France, Spain, or Russia.

Beset by foul weather, Cook failed to observe either the mouth of the Columbia River or the entry to the Strait of Juan de Fuca, the latter being the entrance to Puget South. He did, however, discover and enter Nootka Sound on the east shore of Victoria Island, which he assumed was part of the mainland. There he dropped anchor, remaining for a month or so as his ships were repaired and while he and his officers compiled a detailed report on the character of the natives and the attributes of the land upon which they lived. Oddments of equipment, blankets, and trinkets were traded, especially for sea otter pelts that were abundant on shore, and which the crew used for coats and bedding.

By May 1778, the *Resolution* and the *Discovery* had toured the Aleutian Islands, passed through the Bering Strait and entered Arctic waters. By mid-summer, the expedition arrived a point a little past 70 degrees. There the two ships ran up against a wall of ice, and after exploring it briefly and narrowly escaping being crushed, Cook realized that it could not be penetrated. With that, he set a course back to the northern Pacific.

The expedition subsequently returned south to a group of islands Cook named the "Sandwich Islands," later the Hawaiian Islands, and there the expedition passed the winter. However, Cook and five members of his crew were killed during a minor military expedition to punish the natives for stealing, which marked an unexpected end to what had been a brilliant career. The two ships, then under the command of Captain Charles Clerke, tried one more time to break through the Arctic ice, but again they failed, so they set a course homeward via the Chinese mainland. There, as they pulled in to Canton (Guangzhou) to replenish supplies, something entirely unexpected happened - the sea otter pelts that had been acquired in North America for mere trinkets sold in Canton for extraordinary sums. When they were gone, Chinese merchants clamored for more. The crew tried to persuade Captain Clerke to return to the Pacific Northwest to pick up more, which he refused to do, but if the expedition was searching for some valuable trade resource, then sea otter pelts definitely fit the bill.

Although Cook's third expedition cost him his life and failed to locate the Northwest Passage, it did succeed in putting the Pacific Northwest on the map. Before long, fur traders and explorers were probing a coast newly mapped and documented by the Admiralty, while other notable Royal Navy expeditions, in particular that of George Vancouver, were mounted to add to the general store of knowledge. It was Vancouver who explored and mapped the Puget Sound, named for his lieutenant Peter Puget. Within two decades of Cook's death, the Pacific Northwest was a known quantity.

Vancouver

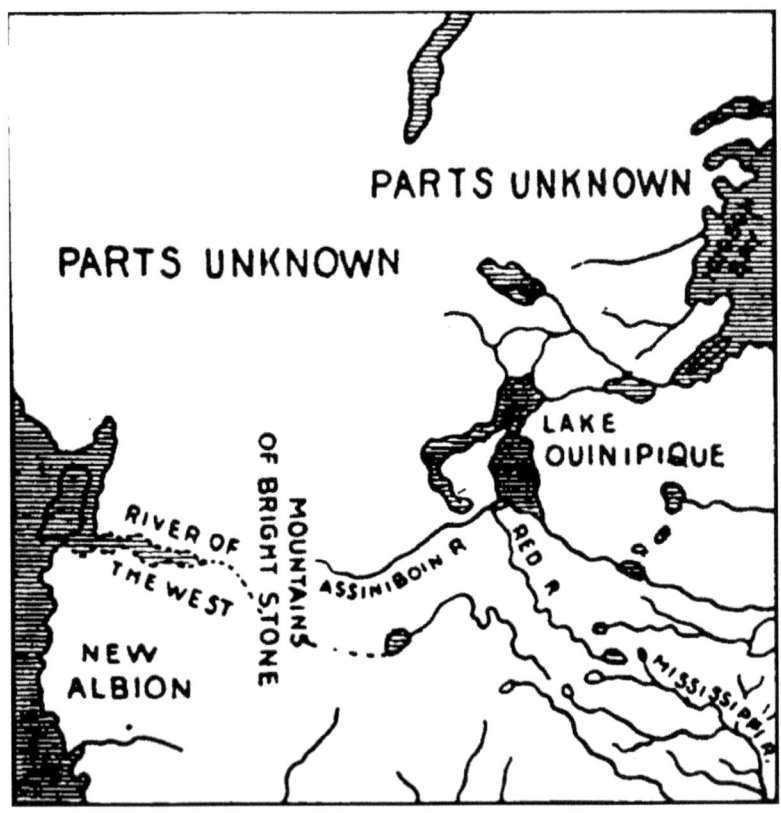

A 1778 map of the region

The Pacific Northwest was the last temperate region on the planet to yield its secrets to European knowledge, but by the 1790s, there were four significant powers present in the region, each with an expressed interest in it. The senior power was Spain, but Russia, Britain and the United States were all poised to develop interests in the region.

The Spanish were given their mandate in 1493 when a proclamation was issued by Pope Alexander VI granting any land not under a Christian ruler to Portugal and Spain. Portuguese mercantile interests at the time were focused on the coast of Africa, the Middle Passage, and the Trans-Atlantic Slave Trade, but it was Spain that left the most profound imprint in the region, even though the Spanish Empire did not devote a lot of resources to any coastal territory north of Mexico. It was from there that tropical trade routes linked Spanish territory in the New World with the Philippines and the European mainland. On behalf of England, Sir Francis Drake peered briefly into the fog, but beyond that, he continued to apply himself to plundering the Spanish, which was a far more lucrative enterprise.

What motivated the Spanish to become more proactive in the region was Russia. The impetus of Russian investment in the region adjoining the far east of Siberia was imperial on the one hand, but mercantile on the other. Their greatest interest was the region's furs, and Russian fur traders had been active along the coast of Siberia for more than a century, but it was only towards the end of the reign of Tsar Peter the Great that a concerted effort was made to explore and exploit the land farther east. The possibility that eastern Russia was linked by land to western America remained a definite possibility, and it was Peter the Great who authorized the first expeditions to investigate the general lay of the land beyond the borders of Siberia.

After Peter's death in 1725, it was his widow and successor, Catherine I, who pushed forward the quest, launching within weeks of her ascent to the throne a definitive expedition led by Vitus Bering. Bering would ultimately command two expeditions, the first of which established the existence of a strait between Siberia and Alaska. The second expedition, which was much more elaborate, crossed the Bering Strait, and in 1741 the Russians began a comprehensive and detailed scientific survey. Bering would not survive this expedition, but the Russian flag was raised on the bleak shores of Alaska, which would remain in Russia's possession for more than a century.

Like the Spanish, however, the Russians did not widely publicize their activities in Alaska and along the Pacific Northwest coast. Nonetheless, Russia's presence was enough the galvanize the Spanish, and through the 1760s and 1770s, the Spanish became conspicuously more active in the region of California, reaching as far north as the Queen Charlotte Islands in an expedition mounted in 1774. A year later, the Spanish penetrated as far north as 58 degrees, taking note on the return journey of the mouth of the Columbia River. In 1776, the year that Captain James Cook embarked from England on his final expedition, the Spanish incorporated the settlement of San Francisco, which one day would become one of the most important seaports and cities on the Pacific coast. In 1779, an expedition commanded by Ignacio de Arteaga got as far north as Mount St. Elias.[1] It was at this point that the Spanish and Russians made cautious contact.

This, at least on paper, added a vast new region of America to the Spanish Empire. As the Spanish pressed north, however, and the Russians moved south, Captain James Cook, with the audacity reserved only for a captain of the Royal Navy, made landfall precisely at the junction of these two imperial spheres of influence, poised like a wedge. Cook dropped anchor, stood on the quarterdeck, surveyed the prospects, and was perfectly willing to be the spark that would ignite a major international crisis.

---

[1] Vitus Bering in fact observed the same sight from somewhat further north.

The catalyst of all of this, apart from the imperial ambitions of all three competing powers, was the fur trade. As Cook's men discovered in Canton, the lustrous pelt of the sea otter, the finest that nature could contrive, commanded outrageous profits, and before long traders from many nations were establishing their presence in the region. With that, Nootka Sound became the most important port of call and trading entrepôt on the coast, even as its sovereignty remained unresolved. The competition was mainly between the British and Spanish, and the first Spanish mariner to observe the port, a man named Juan Pérez, did not make a formal claim on behalf of Spain. Instead, he merely recorded a brief description of what he had seen. Cook also made no formal claim, simply because he assumed that the Spanish already had.

By the end of the 1780s, therefore, the Spanish were confident that annexation of the coast up to the point of contact with the Russians was secure. However, mainly because of the fortunes to be made in the fur trade, the British were now apt to challenge them, and the United States, anxious to develop new markets after its separation from Britain, also began to show an interest.

In the summer of 1789, Spain launched an aggressive expedition to occupy Nootka Sound, which immediately outraged British traders and prompted a diplomatic standoff between the two powers. A British merchant ship under the command of Captain James Colnett arrived in the Sound soon afterwards and was promptly seized by the Spanish, after which the British crew was sent to Mexico as prisoners. This was an extremely provocative move, and it placed the two sides near the brink of war. The crisis even engulfed the United States, which feared an imminent advance by British forces in Canada against Spanish Louisiana. The crisis was so critical that it provoked the first Cabinet-level foreign policy debate to be held in the United States under the new Constitution of 1787.

In a sign of the times, the Spanish blinked first, and the British Empire, fast becoming the strongest on the planet, emerged the winner. The Spanish agreed to claim no territory not secured by treaty or immemorial possession, which was, in effect, an almost total capitulation. This was underlined even more absolutely by a Spanish agreement to pay the British compensation for damages done to British interests in Nootka, and in due course, the Spanish began a southerly retreat that would eventually concede all of the territory north of the 42nd Parallel to the United States.

American Exploration in the West

"The object of your mission is to explore the Missouri river, & such principal stream of it, as, by its course & communication with the waters of the Pacific Ocean, whether the Columbia, Oregon, Colorado and/or other river may offer the most direct & practicable water communication across this continent, for the purposes of commerce." – President Thomas Jefferson's instructions to the Lewis and Clark expedition

By the time he came to office as the third president, Thomas Jefferson had long worried about the future of the western U.S., seeing that settlements in the Ohio Valley and lower south relied upon the Mississippi River. France's controls over the region, in his estimation, put the U.S. at a severe disadvantage. His solution proved successful beyond his wildest imagination, for Napoleon did not only sell New Orleans to the U.S, the portion that Jefferson instructed his ministers to make an offer on, but all of "New France," the entire area of Louisiana. Jefferson might have said later that his purchase of the territory "strained" but did not "break" the Constitution, but also should have boasted that, with one stroke, he had removed one less obstacle to American expansionism.

The Louisiana Purchase encompassed all or part of 15 current U.S. states and two Canadian provinces, including Arkansas, Missouri, Iowa, Oklahoma, Kansas, Nebraska, parts of Minnesota that were west of the Mississippi River, most of North Dakota, nearly all of South Dakota, northeastern New Mexico, northern Texas, the portions of Montana, Wyoming, and Colorado east of the Continental Divide, and Louisiana west of the Mississippi River, including the city of New Orleans. (parts of this area were still claimed by Spain at the time of the Purchase.) In addition, the Purchase contained small portions of land that would eventually become part of the Canadian provinces of Alberta and Saskatchewan. The purchase, which doubled the size of the United States, still comprises around 23% of current U.S. territory.

The purchase was a vital moment in Jefferson's presidency. At the time, it faced domestic opposition as being possibly unconstitutional, and though he felt that the U.S. Constitution did not contain any provisions for acquiring territory, Jefferson decided to purchase Louisiana because he felt uneasy about France and Spain having the power to block American trade access. Jefferson also decided to allow slavery in the acquired territory, which laid the foundation for the crisis of the Union a half century later. On the other hand, Napoleon Bonaparte was looking for ways to finance his empire's expansion, and he also had geopolitical motives for the deal. Upon completion of the agreement, Bonaparte stated, "This accession of territory affirms forever the power of the United States, and I have given England a maritime rival who sooner or later will humble her pride."

The purchase also allowed Jefferson to plan something he had talked about since taking office: an expedition deep into the unmapped and largely unknown continent, with the final destination being the Pacific Ocean. Even before the Louisiana Purchase, and against the advice of those who expected that France and Spain would object, Jefferson had already planned to send Meriwether Lewis and a team through the lands claimed by France and Spain. The historical body of scholarship is united in its appraisal of how, "[t]he political climate in 1803 complicated Jefferson's request." "He had asked Congress to authorize a military reconnaissance into unknown lands that already were claimed by the two most powerful nations in the world, France and Britain, with a third, Spain, clinging to a hold in the south and far west. Jefferson already had approached Spanish officials administering the region on behalf of France, seeking their approval to pass through the Louisiana Territory for the purposes of exploration. Spanish ambassador Don Carlos Martinez objected, but Jefferson pressed ahead with his request to Congress."

With the Louisiana territory squarely in American possession, Jefferson could now embark upon his great plan. In their own way, Meriwether Lewis and William Clark could bring something to the expedition that would offset the problems Jefferson saw developing in America's "wild west" of the late 18th and early 19th centuries. Between the Appalachians and the Mississippi, Americans rapidly filled up the land, and historians have taken note about the state of the colonists in the region: "The half-million Americans (one out of 10) who already lived west of the Appalachian Mountains, however, felt they had found their own "national" interests. Since water routes were viewed as a source of commerce, many people along the Mississippi viewed themselves as the seeds of an independent nation that would tap into the world marketplace, not by going east to the Atlantic seaboard, but by following the Ohio and Mississippi river system down to the Gulf of Mexico." [2]

Thus, Jefferson was anxious about the American settlers on the frontier who might drift away from the Republic. Kingmakers and men of destiny could prove to be the worst thing the U.S. faced, and his own vice-president (Aaron Burr) would serve as the most stunning example, but of even greater concern was the quality of American settlements in the West. Jefferson wanted to spread American civilization and Republican institutions, not merely seed the wilderness with American stock. The way to approach the problem was to enrich the fortunes of the American settlers of this new vast territory. He had meant to do that by taking control of the Mississippi and New Orleans, knowing that their fortunes lay with access to trade and the ability to sell their products.

It's hard to determine exactly what Jefferson had in mind with Native Americans, especially what he thought of their future, and perhaps what challenges they might present to an expanded Republic. However, he still had to deal with the present. "The West was not simply a blank slate during the early years of the Republic. The Indian peoples who inhabited the region constituted formidable obstacles to the progress of American settlement. But they also possessed invaluable information about the continent and its resources that Jefferson and his countrymen sought to exploit."[3]

Thus, from 1804-1806, the first expedition across the North American continent was commissioned by Jefferson and led by Lewis and Clark to traverse the continent until they reached the Pacific, studying everything from the ecology to geography along the way to get an

---

[2] "Circa 1803 (Living in America)." Lewis and Clark: The Journey of the Corps of Discovery, A Film by Ken Burns. http://www.pbs.org/lewisandclark/inside/idx_cir.html (accessed November 3, 2012).

[3] Onuf, Peter S. "Thomas Jefferson and the Expanding Union." *Lewis and Clark: Journal to Another America*, edited by Alan Taylor Missouri Historical Society Press (2003): 165

understanding of the country's new region. In fact, Lewis and Clark would find far more than they bargained for. The 33 men who made the trip came into contact with about two dozen Native American tribes, many of whom helped the men survive the journey, and along the way they met and were assisted by the famous Sacagawea, who would become one of the expedition's most famous participants. Though they suffered deaths on their way west, the group ultimately reached the Pacific coast and got back to St. Louis in 1806, having drawn up nearly 150 maps and giving America a good idea of much of what lay west.

Lewis and Clark

Just by the diligent efforts of collecting samples and cataloguing their observations, the Corps of Discovery made major contributions to the field of science, particularly in determining the geography of the place. Lewis and Clark did so with the production of dozens of maps that marked "their progress and meticulously recorded geographical detail as a guide to locating sites more precisely...The result revolutionized American notions of geography in general and of the West in particular." In essence, the continent became knowable and its accuracy served the interests of national ambitions. Making accurate maps accomplished just that, especially when "Clark made it clear that there existed no easy river-and-portage route to the Pacific." In this way, the failure to locate the fabled Northwest Passage did not end the dream of a route to the riches of the "Orient," but instead replaced them with a new map, where the new "orient" had been discovered in America's West. When "Clark recognized the presence of the American Indian and - significantly - recorded it on his maps," he created a new location for riches that American settlers could aspire towards in the great westward movements of the 19th century. While "it would take many more expeditions to disabuse Americans of such ideas," the maps produced by the expedition ensured future American settlers could become the masters of the continent. Accuracy served imperial ambitions, and "Lewis and Clark had made that possible."[4]

In kind, one goal of the expedition involved the ambitions to control or at least establish relations with Native American tribes as a source of trade and commerce throughout the Mississippi Valley and the regions beyond all the way to the Pacific Ocean. "In 1808, Territorial Governor Lewis wrote a revealing treatise on 'governing the Indian nations' of the West and conducting 'trade and intercourse with the same.' He proposed strict, even coercive, policies designed to regulate white traders through official licenses; to thwart foreign competition through government factories."[5] These were grand designs, as it went without saying that the government's attempt to regulate trade on the frontiers was ambitious. Even disregarding the tendencies of the far-flung colonists living on the periphery, the great distances across the continent proved problematic for these ambitions. No matter what the freedom-living settlers wanted, Lewis sought an officially regulated trade with Native Americans, seeing it as a formative step in the process of federal control over its imperial peripheries. Even more ambitious was his attempt to claim "full sovereignty over all aspects of life in the West."[6]

Jefferson had hoped commerce could be established by the efforts of the expedition through exploration and contact with natives, and both were established. The group discovered the best ways of passage through the terrain and established ways for future American settlers to travel from one distant point to another to trade. And of course, the expedition helped make contact with dozens of different tribes and descriptions of their similarities and differences. Lewis and Clark deserve recognition for accomplishing what Jefferson set out for them to do, "the critical first survey of distant Indian Country, and their greatest legacy was in publicizing and promoting the prospects for western profits among their fellow citizens."[7]

While America's historical memory of the expedition waned by the end of the century, the exploration made important contributions to the successive periods of expansion into the American West, contributions that can be qualified by the successes of American colonists and U.S. military conquest that came after the purchase of Louisiana. No one publicly claimed an "inheritance" won by Lewis and Clark, and there was no real proclamation of ownership over land, but there was a gradual expansion of control as white settlers pushed west. Westward movements displayed fitful starts and stops, and it would be another generation before Americans spoke about Manifest Destiny, but the Corps of Discovery did validate earlier notions of perceived American hegemony over the continent.

---

[4] Konig, David Thomas. "Thomas Jefferson's Scientific Project and the American West." *Lewis and Clark: Journal to Another America, edited by Alan Taylor,* Missouri Historical Society Press (2003): 42-43.
4
[5] 137
[6] 137
[7] Fausz, J. Frederick. "Pacific Intentions: Lewis and Clark and the Western Fur Trade." *Lewis and Clark: Journal to Another America, edited by Alan Taylor,* Missouri Historical Society Press (2003): 135.

Commercial Empires

"Go West, young man." – Horace Greely

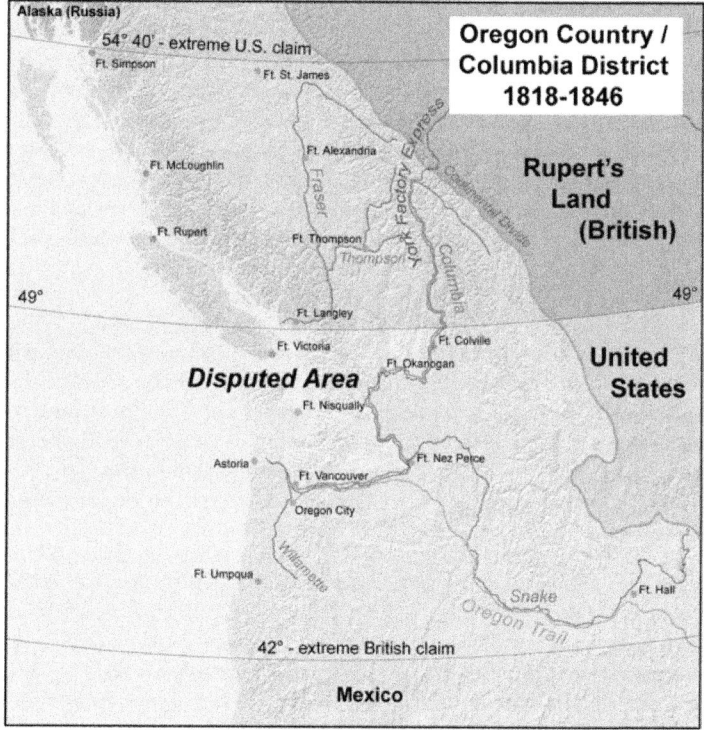

A map of the Pacific Northwest depicting the territorial claims

The 18th century witnessed the rise of the middle-class and the subsequent massive acceleration in demand for luxuries that in the past had been only for kings, the nobility and the wealthy. Furs were among these, and besides sea otter and other garment furs, beaver pelts fashioned into broad-brimmed stovepipe hats generated a sudden demand for that commodity. The rise of the trade in the New World coincided with its decline in much of Europe, with a subsequent shift of capital and a vast expansion of investment in North America.

The hatting industry attracted much legislative debate and, as the emerging major supplier of the world's finest furs, the Hudson's Bay Company was often at the center of discussion. Before the 1690 re-chartering, English hatters, who wanted to obtain their raw materials at the lowest prices possible, convinced parliament to place stricter rules for sales on the Company. The results were that the Company was required to have a public sale of pelts in London between two and four times a year. The sale would take place by auction, and the pelts were required to be sold in relatively small quantities, a requirement requested by the small hat makers who wanted access to the Hudson Bay furs. The pelts were sold at candle auctions, a way of setting the closing of the bids. The highest bidder at the moment a candle, lit at the outset of the auction, went out would win the lot.[8] It is a testament to the Hudson's Bay Company's almost immediate and growing importance to the fur trade that the industries of England were so quickly affected. In terms of volume, the Company produced a steady stream of desirable pelts that kept English manufacturers, as well as their competitors, busy. While much can be said about the company's decisions regarding trade post locations, commitment to quick turnaround times for ships heading to England, and the credit made available to traders who worked to make contact with Indian groups, it is the Indian groups that came to the trade posts seeking goods that delivered the actual goods that the rest of the world desired.

Much of the history concerning early trade relations with the Indians of the region relies on manufacturing records and correspondence since neither the early French traders nor Indian groups maintained written histories or records of their transactions.[9] Rather than painting the tribes who traded with the English and French simplistically as victims being cheated or taken advantage of, Carlos and Lewis focused on this correspondence to reveal the Crees, Assiniboine, Dakotas, and Chipewyans[10] as equal players in the supply and demand transactions taking place in both New France and in Rupert's Land.

In 1684, the York Factory post, built at the mouth of the Hayes River, was established. The post, attracting Indian traders who could access it by canoe, became a major center of commerce, and therefore, an object of great desire for the French. The post was taken by the French and re-taken by the English multiple times between the time of its establishment and 1713, when the Peace of Utrecht officially granted the post to the British. The Indian populations surrounding the area remained relatively small due to the harsh weather conditions of the north and disease. It can be estimated that about 8,600 Indians, including all active tribes in the region, occupied the lands served by the York Company post.[11]

For many decades, the York post functioned as a place of reception, rather than exploration. Each summer Indians arrived in small groups, ready to conduct trade. It was not until 1774, when the Hudson's Bay Company began to establish its posts in the interior as well as along waterways, that they understood the effect independent traders were having on the fur supply. Though at first the competition was from independent traders that the British called "pedlars,"

---

[8] Carlos and Lewis, 29.
[9] Ibid., 69.
[10] Ibid., 70
[11] Ibid., 72.

the company's greatest competitor was the Northwest Company.[12] Because the Hudson's Bay outposts initially concentrated efforts on trade and not exploration, it could be said that the Indians exerted greater control over the actual trade process than the Europeans, who were eventually frustrated with the wait and ventured out themselves to create further trade opportunities.

A depiction of trade with Indians at a post

Trade was not only an economic exchange, but also a social one. Indian groups liked the

---

[12] "Our History: Acquisitions: Fur Trade: The North West Company." *Hudson's Bay Company Heritage.* Accessed December 19, 2016.

formality and ceremony of a pre-business gift exchange. Here, the native trade leader and the governors of the post would meet outside following an announcement by initial Indian gunfire and a response of cannon and flag-raising by the fort. The native leader was often presented with a suit of clothing and his fellow traders with food goods and tobacco. In return the governors would be presented with pelts. After additional ceremony, actual trade took place at the post's warehouse, where the native leader would enter for negotiations.[13] The rest of the Indian traders were to remain outside, trading through the post's windows while they waited for their leader to emerge.

The Metis people, later one of the three recognized aboriginal groups in Canada, were an Indian group that came from marriages between French traders and Indian women, but Scotch and English cultures were also heavy influencers among the Metis. The term comes from a Latin word for "to mix" and originally referred to the children of these relationships. The Metis would grow to become a major intermediary between the governors of Rupert's Land and the Indian traders with the Company, and after 1800, "considered themselves a separate nation, different from other people, including the Indians and the French."[14]

---

[13] Carlos and Lewis, 73.
[14] Peter Bakker, *A Language of Our Own: The Genesis of Michif, the Mixed Cree-French Language of the Canadian Métis* (New York: Oxford University Press, 1997), 28.

A Metis trader

As trade developed in Rupert's Land, a medium of exchange became desirable. When officers of the Company or traders met up with Indians who had furs to trade, a post was not always nearby and the goods desired by the Indians might not be in stock in that post. A system of coinage, then, was developed that would not only allow the Indians to be "paid" for their pelts immediately, but also allow them to spend the money later. The first coins were made of ivory, wood, or shell and were known as Made Beaver coins. The name came from the idea that the value of one coin corresponded with the price of a perfect adult beaver pelt, which simplified trade and relieved the load of goods that traders would need to carry on their person. Now that purchases could be made later, the pelt portion of the transaction could carry on while the natives saved their money for a convenient time to buy. So widely used were the coins that goods eventually became known as having a value in Made Beaver (MB). Brass and aluminum tokens eventually replaced the wood, shell, and ivory, and eventually, Fox coins came to replace Beaver coins. Not only did the Hudson's Bay issue coins, but their competitor, the Northwest Company produced its own Made Beaver coins. As with any tool that makes transactions easier and faster, the Made Beaver coins not only regulated the fur trading industry and its prices, it also provided stability for many of the tradesman who had a standard of value when conducting transactions.[15]

The fur trade had its tensions, but for many years, traders and natives worked out their own systems, times, and traditions, allowing many different groups to interact and even compete without issues that led to war. Though Indian groups sometimes found themselves in conflicts based on long-standing rivalries or relations with the Europeans, most of the fur traders, the trappers, the Indians, and Company officials lived peaceably. The great amount of distance from one another in this land of millions of miles likely helped to alleviate tensions. When a new vision for the Hudson's Bay came about, one where settlers, not itinerants, would be responsible for the colony, the rules changed.

In time, the Hudson's Bay Company began to operate like a virtual empire within an empire, and it held an almost absolute monopoly on trade across most of British North America. From the 1780s onwards, however, it faced vigorous competition from a new rival in the form of the North West Company of Montreal. Blocked out of the most lucrative fur regions of British North America, the North West Company established itself in the Pacific Northwest and pushed aggressively westward, creating the first European settlements and outposts among the native tribes of the Columbia territory. In part, President Jefferson's objective in sponsoring the Lewis and Clark Expedition was to find a way to direct this growing trade into the United States, rather than north into British territory or west across the ocean. As Lewis and Clark returned to St. Louis, the North West Company was already exploring New Caledonia, comprising most of modern-day British Columbia. None of this was formal British territory, of course, but along with most of the coast above the 42nd Parallel, it formed part of Britain's claim, and the companies active therein tended to reinforce this fact.

In 1808, North West Company explorer Alexander Mackenzie traced the great Canadian river now bearing his name to the Arctic Ocean, disappointed that it did not empty, as expected, into the Pacific Ocean. This, however, was further incentive to look south and west, and at about the same time, North West Company trader and explorer David Thompson undertook a series of journeys of exploration that opened up a vast new territory comprising the upper Columbia River, British Columbia, Idaho and Montana.

From the other direction came the first significant figure representing American commerce, John Jacob Astor, a brash German immigrant destined to become the wealthiest man in America. At the age of 17, Astor moved to London to work for his eldest brother, George, a manufacturer of musical instruments. Three years later, he departed for the U.S. to seek his fortune, in possession of a few flutes and $25.00. Arriving at the port of Baltimore, he soon migrated north to New York City to join his brother, Henry. In 1785, he married Sarah Cox Todd, with whom he would raise seven children. In the following year, one decade after the signing of Jefferson's Declaration of Independence, Astor established his first fur shop, often going into the wilderness

---

[15]"HBC Fur Trade Tokens." Manitoba Government Archives. <http://www.gov.mb.ca>

himself to guarantee that it remained well stocked. Within a few years, he found his calling in the larger fur and shipping trades, aptly demonstrating an intent to go well beyond the status of a provincial merchant. "Astute and pragmatic," the ambitious and at times ruthless Astor owned more than a dozen ships by the turn of the century. Not yet having reached the age of 30, he was already trading in China for tea, opium, and a number of other products not native to the American continent.

Astor

Astor's imagination concocted and perfected the vision of a multi-directional flow of trade, with products crossing the continent from New York to Oregon, where he had already purchased property by 1806. The fur products would be sent on to several eastern points. Return trips would bring all manner of exotic Asian products to eastern American and European cities. On the periphery were numerous tribes of the Pacific Northwest, furnishing Astor's company with furs in return for cheaply obtained blankets and beads. Similarly, an additional source of beaver, otter, and other fur-bearing animals was to come from Russian America (present-day Alaska) through Archangelsk (now the city of Sitka). The Russians greatly preferred American business to that of European enterprises and were particularly hopeful that Britain would be pushed out of the region due to political strife between the two countries.

In addition to carefully building his companies, Astor watched the competition with a keen eye and learned a great deal from the establishment of the North West Company. The personnel of the various fur companies in the New World often kept close company. In the unpopulated wild, they depended on one another as protection against isolation and even collaborated in some circumstances. However, Astor wanted a monopoly on the Pacific Northwest, where all trade with the Indians could be carried out through one company. To accomplish that, he had to accelerate Jefferson's thinking and begin the process quickly before the North West Company caught wind of it and intruded.

Well aware of the report brought back by Lewis and Clark, and aware of the British presence in the Great Lakes region, Astor went to work by soliciting the help of New York City Mayor DeWitt Clinton. Clinton's uncle served as the Vice President to Jefferson, and therefore, he had the president's ear. Astor also maintained a good relationship with Albert Gallatin, Secretary of the Treasury for the first decade of the century.

Clinton

Gallatin

Before long, Astor was able to write freely to Jefferson, who was a famously avid correspondent. Rather than providing the president with volumes of economic forecasts and speculative ledgers, he stressed the political requirements of gaining a hold on the American West. He preyed upon Jefferson's desire for expansion and his hopes for full American coffers through trade as well. Astor reminded the president of the Lewis and Clark reports, and the two developed a vision of one company's monopoly over the fur trade in its one-sided partnership with the tribes. Its operations, supply, and trade routes were all to be kept under one sphere of influence in order to prevent a European bidding war or actual military intrusion for tribal allegiances. In such a scenario, peace on the continent was to be more easily preserved, and international partnerships were rendered unnecessary, outside of clients. For Jefferson's part, expansion and eventual annexation of the western portion of the continent would come at no public cost, taking the contested land simply through a greater degree of occupation and infusion of resident industry than that of his rivals. Astor's idea, as expressed to Jefferson, went so far as to push the British out of both the Great Lakes and the Pacific Northwest entirely. More than protecting trade, the vision offered Jefferson a greater sense of security on the borders.

The anti-British sentiment was expressed with full knowledge that British goods were needed for trade with the tribes. The only legal obstacle was the recently passed Embargo Act, which forbade the acquisition of British goods in the U.S. Britain was at war with France, and both countries habitually stopped American merchant ships to check for weapons shipments and European crewmen. The Embargo Act was Jefferson's "nonviolent resistance"[16] and an expression of insistence on American rights in the trading world. The Embargo Act was passed in 1806, but it was delayed a year until a British warship fired on and detained the American warship *Leopold*.

Despite the acquisition of a charter for Astor's new company being easily obtained from Clinton, the Act hovered over his ability to start the project. Eventually, all of his ventures, including the Southwest Fur Company and the newly created Pacific Fur Company, were placed under the umbrella of the American Fur Company in 1808. The Embargo Act was revoked in 1809 in the final days of the Jefferson administration, and Astor was prepared for immediate action. However, Monroe continued such practices as an embargo against Britain in the following years, creating the tension leading up to the War of 1812. That conflict came to carry serious consequences for the Astor/Jefferson experiment. For the time being, however, Astor had secured the president's blessing.

In 1810, through the Pacific Fur Company, Astor began to direct his energies at the still mostly unexploited regions accessible from the mouth of the Columbia River. This was, of course, in open defiance of British claims, but that was very much in keeping with Astor's style. Astor put up the money, and a group of American and Canadian fur traders managed affairs on the ground.

Astor's plunge into the Pacific Northwest took the form of two expeditions, one overland from the east and the other by water. The latter comprised 33 Canadians and Scotsmen, as well as a fortune in trade goods and equipment, all stacked in the holds of the *Tonquin*, a 290 ton merchant ship that sailed from New York in September 1810. Thousands of miles later, the *Tonquin* arrived at the mouth of the Columbia River, encountering the same atrocious weather conditions that met Drake, Cook, and Lewis and Clark before it. At the cost of 8 crewmen lost in the attempt, the *Tonquin* beat a passage to a protected cove on the south bank of the river where Fort Astoria was established. This was the basis of the port city that bears the same name today.

The essence of Astor's scheme was to use the *Tonquin* to trade furs with China, but in a curious twist in the story, the *Tonquin* disappeared while trading for furs with the native tribes around Nootka Bay. What happened to the ship remains a mystery, but natives of the area later reported that Captain Jonathan Thorn, a disreputable character, adopted an antagonistic and aggressive attitude to those he was trading with on shore, and at some point, the ship was overrun and all aboard were massacred.

---

[16] *Encyclopaedia Britannica, The Embargo Act of 1807* – www.encyclopaediabritannica.co.uk

A depiction of the *Tonquin*

Whatever might have been the truth, when the *Tonquin* disappeared, so did Astor's ambitions to seal up the Pacific Northwest fur trade, because the overland expedition fared no better. Placed in command was Wilson Price Hunt, a 27 year old native of St. Louis who had no experience when it came to a journey on that scale. As a consequence, the expedition degenerated almost immediately into a hunger march across a vast expanse of wilderness that claimed quite a number of lives and certainly did not forge a bold passage across the Great Divide for the direction of future trade.

While the settlement at Astoria made preparations to explore the interior and set up connecting posts, the international competition increased. By now, American claims were becoming more tangible, especially after Captain Robert Gray's exploration of the Columbia River 30 miles into the interior. Gray, a Bostonian, not only sailed upriver, but established the first American trading relationship with lower Columbia tribes. The Chinook proved to be essential to facilitating the Pacific Fur Company's progress with fellow tribes farther to the interior, although they were never considered entirely reliable.

Gray

The Chinook of the lower Columbia were under the authority of Chief Concomly. Through his admonitions and conversations with neighboring tribes, he was able to regulate the Astorians' progress and change the state of relations quickly. Regardless, the Astorians owed much to Concomly, who understood trade with the west, having met Lewis and Clark. In the first meetings, the Astorians were received with generous hospitality. In addition, he saved the lives of two Astorian leaders in an early visit to their village on the northern Columbian shore. He warned Stuart and MacDougall that the waves were too high to return to Astoria in their small boat, but the two set out anyway, over 11 miles of open bay. Capsizing in the current, they were saved by Concomly's "timely succor,"[17] as the chief arrived in a light canoe to save them. While recuperating in the village until the tide changed, Concomly offered every entertainment for the stranded trappers. The women took great interest in the Europeans, anointing themselves with fish oil and decorating themselves with red clay. Although such forms of seduction might have been off-putting to those of a typically European culture, the Chinook women's efforts succeeded with MacDougall, who married one of Concomly's daughters soon after. For Chief Concomly, marrying his daughter to an Astorian "increased his access"[18] to British goods. For MacDougall and the settlement, such a connection enhanced "economic and physical security."[19]

---

[17] *Revolvy*

[18] *Revolvy*

Seduction was not the Astorians' only purpose in contact with Chinook women. The Europeans soon learned that women were expert traders and essential to the negotiation process in all Chinook business. This required an altered world view in the Astorians' business dealings.

Chief Concomly

The Chinook were not always willing to work as guides or messengers to other tribes situated at great distances. Through this reluctance, they often delayed the Astorians from making important introductions before the North West Company intruded and undermined them. On one occasion, the tribe escorted Francois Benjamin Pillet up the Columbia a short way, but abruptly refused to go any farther after small exchanges with the Skilloots near the mouth of the Cowlitz River. He made the dubious declaration that seasonal flooding would prohibit further travel, and Pillet was forced to return to the settlement. Nevertheless, Astoria placed great importance on retaining the Lower Chinook as the resident middlemen. Concomly provided Astoria with fish once the ceremonial catches were complete. Salmon was a basic source of nutrition, and the Hawaiian talent for fishing was put to good use as a "constant task"[20] while the salmon were in

---

[19] *Revolvy*

[20] *Revolvy*

season. The Europeans, however, grew discontented with a fish-based diet. Roosevelt elk and black-tailed deer were seen from time to time, but not in large enough numbers for a reliance on a steady supply of meat. Concomly introduced the settlement to wapato root, an important staple for the winter. An excellent substitute for potatoes, they were brought in such quantity that storage cellars had to be built. The Chinook displayed a talent for weaving, and trappers purchased tightly interwoven hats to keep out the cold. Not only was the weaving waterproof, but wide enough to cover the shoulders. As a peripheral attraction, expertly woven animal images were included in the texture. Whether these images carried a spiritual significance or expressed an artistic bent is unknown.

Despite the Pacific Fur Company's success with Concomly and the Lower Chinooks, Britain's North West Company solidified its hold on the market through the establishment of numerous inland posts, such as the Spokane House, Kootenai House, and Saleesh House. These were located far up the Columbia where it turns directly toward the north, hundreds of miles from Astoria. However, it was a region to be exploited, and the Americans immediately affirmed their intention to build there as well. Almost immediately, they responded with a flanking maneuver by soliciting a trade connection with Russian America more rapidly than expected. The effort resulted in a "beneficial agreement"[21] by which Russia would greatly augment American trading supplies. The agreement was intended to prevent Montreal's presence in the region. Russia's distaste for such a close British presence was a boon for Astor's company's dealings with the far north. From colonial times, the eastern part of the continent was dominated by the Hudson's Bay Company and several French enterprises. Such was Hudson Bay's scope that were it to stake a claim in the West, it could dominate the entire coast alongside the North West Company. At that point, the British claim to land would take on a stark reality for an American president intent on connecting the two oceans.

Scarcely a month after the *Tonquin*'s arrival, the commercial functions of Fort Astoria were already producing results and establishing a presence in the Columbia Basin as the prospective "Emporium of the West."[22] However, the actual supply and residence structures, situated only a few miles from the Lewis and Clark winter quarters at Fort Clatsop, were barely begun. Terrain and thick forests made clearing the land a Herculean task. The standing timber of the coastal Columbia is thick and tall, with heavy underbrush. Few among the party had ever swung an axe, and none had logging experience. The trees were swathed in hardened resin, slowing progress even further, and removing stumps seemed all but impossible. Typically, four men stood on a platform at least eight feet above the ground to cut each tree, and the slow pace continued at a rate of one tree per two days. The settlement had no resident medical officer, and almost as a rule, one half of the available personnel was unable to work due to a variety of illnesses.

---

[21] *Revolvy*

[22] *Revolvy*

Still, despite the ubiquitous presence of the North West Company, Astor's Pacific Fur Company held the most strategically practical and defendable location in the Pacific Northwest, and such discomforts would not drive them out. The earliest American settlement in the West between Spain's San Francisco and Russian America, Astoria's initial success fit in well with Astor's intent to complement international sea trade via a string of forts across the American continent, using American tribes as suppliers.

As intended, small parties fanned out from Astoria in the following months to establish trade relations with various inland tribes. The first interior routes always began by traveling directly eastward upriver. Within a month or two following Tonquin's arrival, Captain Thorn grew restless to fulfill the ship's part of the bargain and departed for the north coast as per Astor's instructions. On June 5, the day of her departure, only a small part of the settlement had been successfully completed, but Thorn could wait no longer. His itinerary included a voyage all the way to Russian America to meet with Alexander Baranov at New Arkhangel (modern-day Sitka). There, he was to trade supplies and a large number of gunpowder barrels before returning to the Columbia and on to foreign markets.

Of the new posts built throughout the region, one of the nearest to Astoria was the Wallace House of what is now Keizer, Oregon, in the Salem area of the Willamette Valley. Also known under the name of Fort Calapooya after the local tribe, Wallace House became an important source for beaver pelt and much-needed venison to feed the Columbia settlement. Unlike Astoria, the Willamette Valley was abundant in elk and white-tailed deer. Wallace House was founded by a party of 14, led by William Wallace and John Haisley, and the group wintered over in the valley, returning to Astoria almost two years later with nearly 800 beaver pelts. What the residents of Wallace House did not expect was an entire new spate of allergies and diseases that thrive in the Oregon country's high humidity. The Willamette Valley was dubbed by tribes who had lived there for centuries as the "valley of a thousand fevers," and European descendants often had difficulty coping with the natural conditions. Astoria itself fared scarcely better, with the cold, humidity, and alien features of the environment.

Of the distant posts, among the most prominent was the fort established at the confluence of the Columbia and the Okannakken (in modern usage, Okanogan). To reach the junction, the first party took 42 grueling days, but the established facility became the first such post built by Americans in the future state of Washington. This was Astor's response to the North West Company's Spokane House and other northeastern posts. The North West Company enjoyed a two-year advantage over him in the area, building its impressive facility close to modern-day Spokane. Rival companies often built their posts in proximity to one another without heightened tensions. All understood that the same resources were sought, regardless of the post's location. Companies often preferred to have the competition situated nearby for social interaction through the long seasons. However, in the case of Fort Okanogan, opposite North West's Spokane House, a council was held with the leaders of the Okanogan tribe, and an official agreement was forged in order to maintain friendly relations. Under ordinary circumstances, this might not have been necessary. However, far to the east, tensions were rising between Britain and the U.S. that would result in a coming war. The council was well worth the trouble, as the American group produced a harvest of 2,500 beaver pelts by the following spring.

Fort Okanogan

Jon Roanhaus' picture of the site of the fort

Relations between traders and regional tribes varied greatly. Perhaps the most welcoming and cordial relationship was with the Syilx at the mouth of the Okannakken. Astorians, in fact, received an official invitation from the tribe to live with them as members of the community. The message was delivered by Kauxama Nupika, described by her tribe as a "two-spirit." Kauxama was a woman of extremely tall, muscular stature who claimed that the supernatural powers of the white man had changed her into a male. She took a wife and engaged in male roles and rituals, including horse stealing and fighting. It is ironic that her message to the Astorians was an invitation for a peaceful life, despite her reputation for sudden, unexpected violence.

Even for the Chinook guides and interpreters, communication with the Syilx and their Nysilxcom language was problematic. The Okanogan Trail followed by the Astorians was known to the Syilx as Nkwala's Trail in honor of their chief. The tribal invitation invited the trappers to live in the large native encampment or to build a trading post, with the accompanying exhortation to "always be our friends."[23]

---

[23] *Revolvy*

Not all inland trade routes emanating from Astoria involved following the Columbia. To the north were as many unfamiliar tribes as there were to the east. On May 12, 1811, David Stuart led a party with the assistance of Calpo, a Clatsop guide, northward after a brief trek east up the Columbia. In the settlement's first departure from the Columbia, Stuart explored the Cowlitz River and at one bend encountered a massive flotilla of Cowlitz warriors. MacKay was able to successfully achieve parlay and learned that the gathering had armed itself for combat against the nearby Skilloot village, near the river's mouth. The Stuart party was, for the time being, safe. Meanwhile, in the same week, the group moving eastward up the river arrived in what is now The Dalles. There, they discovered the most important fishery of the entire river, what was later known as Celilo Falls, eventually lost to the Dalles Dam. The Dalles struck the expedition as one of the most ideal spots on the river for a trading fort, and they were shocked that no one had ever attempted it. Despite the opportunity, they were forced to retreat back to Astoria, as Calpo would not continue. He feared reprisals against him and his people from the Wishram-Wasco tribe.

In early June, Stuart led another party north along the coast of present-day Washington, again with Calpo leading the way. The party reached the Olympic Peninsula with its high mountain range, where Stuart spoke with several tribal leaders. Most were subsets of the large coastal Salishan nation extending from the Columbia to Vancouver Island and inland to Puget Sound. The languages, however, differed in each region. Stuart's party returned to Astoria within three weeks with good news from the Quinault and Quileute. These two tribes offered to kill sea otters and trade pelts for valuable Dentalium shells commonly sold by the Nuuchalnulth on Vancouver Island. Stuart was desirous of a new trading post at what is now Gray's Harbor on the northern coast. He had good reason to believe that the Alutiiq, as far north as Russian America, could be recruited to hunt various fur-bearing animals as well. These could easily be sent to the southern factory of Astoria for preparation and shipping.

The War of 1812, although mostly fought on the other side of the continent, impacted events in the Pacific region profoundly. The war was ended by the Treaty of Ghent, and a clause of the agreement allowed for the restoration of all territory taken during the conflict, including that which was seized from the Astorians. Fort George was no more, Spain had retreated behind what is now the border of California and Oregon, and Russia remained north of the 54th Parallel. In essence, the only contestants remaining in the tug-of-war for the Oregon Country were Britain and the United States.[24] The territorial boundaries remained loosely defined, and theoretically open to be settled by anyone.

As for Astor, his wealth continued to grow as the war drew to a close, in part through a lucrative bond deal forged with the U.S. government. The loss of Astoria caused no small amount of frustration to its namesake, but it was not overly significant in financial terms. His

---

[24] The origin of the name "Oregon" is obscure, but it is generally attributed to the Spanish, with origins as diverse as the proliferation of oregano in the southern parts, and a reference made to "orejón" in the historic chronicle *Relación de la Alta y Baja California*, written in 1598 by the new Spaniard Rodrigo Motezuma.

New York City investments skyrocketed, and the parent American Fur Company was eventually sold.

This turn of events left the North West Company largely in the driver's seat at a time when decreasing revenues were forcing the company to widen its search for new fur trading regions. This would lead to a de facto hot war with the Hudson's Bay Company, and things became so heated that in 1821, the British Colonial Secretary forced an amalgamation of the two. By dint of seniority, it was the North West Company that was absorbed into the Hudson's Bay Company, which now encompassed millions of square miles, tens of thousands of employees and hundreds of trade depots, forts and factories.

Even today, it is astonishing to consider that a region comprising about 3 million square miles fell under the control of a private company and board of directors based in London, so it should come as no surprise that Hudson's Bay Company officials were unsure what to do. The extent of the company's holdings often outstripped its administrative capacity, and its leaders had very mixed feelings about the acquisition of the Oregon Country as a huge additional asset. The region still had unproven potential, and thanks to a generally milder winter climate, it was understood that the quality of furs sourced in this region were inferior to those of the far north. There was a substantial body of opinion within the company in favor of abandoning the area altogether, but a majority remained interested in giving the region the benefit of the doubt. At the same time, everyone was aware that the land was still potentially up for dispute between Britain and America, which would require the kind of political diplomacy the Hudson's Bay Company could not practically engage in.

One of the most influential men of the Hudson's Bay Company in the first half of the 19th century, and an exception to this rule, was Sir George Simpson, director of North American operations. At a time when the British were consolidating an empire across the globe, Simpson combined great imperial vision with a genius for company administration. As a young executive officer, he was charged with determining the pattern of administration of the company's interests in the Pacific Northwest. Furthermore, he acknowledged that the Columbia River would likely form a future international boundary, and that the presence of a British fort on the southern bank of the river was not to the advantage of the British Empire. If it happened that the territory was divided along the line of the Columbia, which seemed inevitable, then a substantial settlement on the north bank would better fortify the overall British position. As a result, Fort George was eventually abandoned, and the British crossed the river and moved 100 miles upstream to the site of present-day Vancouver, Washington, where Fort Vancouver was established.

Simpson

An 1845 depiction of Fort Vancouver

With an eye tuned to both commerce and politics, Simpson channeled more resources to Fort Vancouver than would typically have been the case for a regional depot, and he established numerous satellite trading posts in the Snake River Country. To manage it all, he appointed Dr. John McLoughlin, a towering figure in the early administration of the area, and a man of striking appearance and vivid personality. Originally from Quebec and of mixed Irish and Scottish heritage, McLoughlin was precisely the right type of man to keep command of an unruly territory unserved by any official agency or officer of the law. From 1824-1846, McLoughlin ruled the extensive Columbia Department with an iron fist, answerable only to a distant regional headquarters. Put simply, he wielded extraordinary power.

In the meanwhile, as part of an ongoing program to reinforce the British presence north of the Columbia, a subsidiary company, the Puget Sound Agricultural Company, was formed to spearhead farming enterprises in an area south of modern-day Tacoma. Fort Nisqually, Fort Colville and Cowlitz Farm were established, producing quantities of livestock and crops in a generally fertile region.

All that was lacking were settlers, and herein lay the difficulty, because the immigrants arriving to take up the task of settling the land were generally American.

Increased Settlement

"There are four great measures for my administration - a reduction of tariff, an independent treasury, settlement of the Oregon boundary and acquisition of California." - President James K. Polk

At the start of the 1840s, the Oregon Country had no political boundaries or effective government. The only administrative organization in the territory was the Hudson's Bay Company, which applied only to British subjects, and aside from natives, the region was populated by a handful of independent traders, hunters, and prospectors, as well as those employed in the various company depots.

The first to begin showing up in large numbers were missionaries. The native populations were by then diminished by disease and dispirited, which meant they were more receptive to missionary aid and the Christian message. Christianity, of course, was not entirely unknown among the indigenous populations, given that marriages between white men and Indian women created a hybrid of "folk" Christianity that was commonly observed among the Indians. The first wave of missionaries represented the American Methodists, arriving in or around 1834, followed a year or two later by a second series of arrivals, sponsored this time by the American Board of Commissioners for Foreign Missions (ABCFM). The ABCFM was an ecumenical organization founded to promote the general outreach of the Presbyterian and Dutch Reform churches in the United States. Roman Catholics arrived around 1830, bringing missionaries mostly from Canada and Europe.

Perhaps the most famous missionary party of this era consisted of a Presbyterian ABCFM missionary group including Marcus Whitman and his wife Narcissa, who established their mission on the confluence of the Walla Walla and Columbia Rivers. The Whitman Mission later became an important staging post on the Oregon Trail. The fortunes of the Whitman Mission, however, became something of an object lesson in race relations in the new territory, ultimately with very tragic results.

The mission was well funded, and its settlement, at least by the standards of native society, was lavish. Initially, the couple and their followers treated the neighboring Cayuse tribe with generosity, distributing material largess as well as medicine and rudimentary education. The relationship between the two parties, however, was complicated, and Marcus Whitman appeared to grow disenchanted with persistent demands for material goods made upon the mission. Eventually, he stopped providing goods, which sowed a certain amount of discontent among the Cayuse, and animosity took root. When an epidemic of measles swept through the community, killing hundreds of natives, they blamed the mission for poisoning them. In November 1847, Marcus and Narcissa Whitman, along with 11 other missionaries, were massacred by a Cayuse war party. That attack would have profound implications not only for the Cayuse and other native tribes of the region, but also for the future direction of the territory.

Meanwhile, more white Americans were moving north via the Oregon Trail. The Oregon Trail was really more like a series of relatively well-known trails that had been utilized by Indians and fur-trappers. For overland migrants, the trick was just connecting these various trails into one route that would take them into the Oregon Territory. Many of the people who created the trails that the wagon trains would follow were fur-trappers like Thomas Fitzpatrick, Joseph Walker, Moses Harris, James Beckwourth, Joe Meek, Kit Carson, Caleb Greenwood and James Clyman. Often, these men worked as part of the U.S. Army's efforts to explore and map the West, but once the initial discovery and trail creation had been occurred, engineers published these findings, which allowed virtually anyone to have access to information about the trail networks.

The literature on the Oregon Trail ranged widely in terms of quality. One of the most important early pieces written on the West was John C. Fremont's Report of the Exploring Expedition to the Rocky Mountains in 1842 which discussed his expedition to the South Pass. While Fremont's book was not written specifically for the wagon trains and had little practical value for them, it did convince many Americans that overland travel West was possible and could be done safely. Less scrupulous authors tried to take advantage of the market for trail guidebooks and published works that could be quite vague. Lansford Hastings' The Emigrants' Guide, to Oregon and California, for example, seemed to provide good information on supplies and equipment for the trip west, but provided almost no worthwhile information on the actual conditions of the trail or what the experience would be like.

It would not be until 1846 that a number of quality guidebooks were published and provided information on the actual conditions and geography of the trail. The most informative books listed important details that western migrants could use for their trip. For example, lists of campsites, trading posts, landmarks, river crossings, and the best routes to take could all be vital to wagon trains. Guidebooks would be important sources of information not only for those on the Oregon Trail but also the California and Mormon Trails as well. As a result, the first wagon trains would be full of people who had little idea just what they were getting themselves into.

When the first wagon train was organized in 1836, the West was still a heavily contested region, and any migrants moving along the Oregon Trail knew full well they would be traveling through "Indian Country," which had been designated as such by Congress in 1834. Indian Country referred to the territory west of the Missouri River, and the land that made up the area between the Great Plains and the Snake River was under the control of various Indian groups. At the same time, Mexico claimed sovereignty over the territory of the Pacific Northwest, even though it was various groups of Indians and the British men of the Hudson's Bay Company who actually lived on that land.

In terms of the route that perspective western migrants took, the geography of the west funneled them into a route that went along the Platte River valley. Once beyond the Great Plains, further geographic barriers funneled travel once more, this time in the form of the Colorado

River's canyon system, and the deserts surrounding the Great Salt Lake. From there, migrants had to cross the Rocky Mountains through the South Pass, the only known easy crossing of the mountain range before the 1880s. Fortuitously, the path laid out by the geography of the west lined up with the South Pass, and once over the Rocky Mountains, travelers had to move across more deserts before making their way through the Cascade Mountains.

Provisions were a constant concern for the wagon trains, and the small number of forts that dotted the Trail were mostly unable to aid travelers. Forts such as Fort John, Fort Hall, and Fort Boise were centered around trade with the Native Americans, so they were stocked only with trade goods and enough supplies for the workers that resided in these locations. Should the wagon trains run out of food along the way, the forts would be no help to them. As James Looney noted in 1841, "There is little or nothing to be had in the way of provisions at the forts on the way."

Travelers moving overland to the Oregon Territory were also a diverse lot, as one wagon train participant wrote in 1857: "Our party consisted of 30 wagons, 300 head of cattle and a lot of hands made up from Mexico, Ireland, England, Wales, France and Germany." This was in addition to the large number of Americans who made the trek from the east to the west, whose reasons were as diverse as their backgrounds. For Belinda Cooley Pickett," I believe that human beings are bound never to feel satisfied." For Antonio B. Rabbeson, "Like many boys who have picked [up] novels I have read of the life of mountaineers. I was very conscious to make a trip across the plains so that I could kill buffalo, etc., deer etc., and have a good time. That was about all of my motive - a young fellows idea of adventure." Dr. James Middleton wrote, "My greatest pleasure in travelling through the country is derived from the knowledge that it has seldom been traversed, or at least never been described by any hackneyed tourist, that everything I see or look upon has been seen by me before it has become common by the vulgar gaze or description of others."

Perhaps most importantly, unlike many other western migrants, travelers to Oregon had the added push of patriotism because the land there was contested by two nations, According to Miriam Thompson Tuller, "My husband [was] fired with patriotism to help keep the country from British rule, and I was possessed with a spirit of adventure and a desire to see what was new and strange."

At the same time, not everyone viewed the pull of westward migration as a good thing. For army officer Philip St. George Cook, travelers were plagued by "the wantonness of discontent, - a diseased appetite for excitement and change...[and] a restless habit of vagrancy." Ultimately, a frontiersman named James Clyman may have summed it up best while hinting at the same thing Cook did: "It is remarkable...and strange that so many of all kinds and classes of People should sell out comfortable homes in Missouri and Elsewhere pack up and start across such an emmence Barren waste to settle in some new Place of which they have at most so uncertain information but this is the character of my countrymen...all ages and all sects are found to undertake this long tedious and even dangerous Journey for some unknown object never to be realized even by those most fortunate - and why? Because the human mind can never be satisfied [or] at rest [but must be] always on the stretch for something new."

Not surprisingly, those who were willing to travel west were a hardscrabble lot, and commentators who came into contact with the wagon trains along the Oregon Trail frequently took note of the condition and spirit of the people moving west. At Independence, Missouri, Francis Parkman described some travelers as "very sober-looking countrymen," while others were "some of the vilest outcasts in the country." Further along the trail to the west, Edwin Bryant explained that "there was not a man in the country, now that he had left it, who was not as thoroughly steeped in villany as the most hardened graduate of the penitentiary."

On the other hand, people with experience in the West, especially fur trappers and workers at Western forts, thought the people making up the wagon trains were woefully inexperienced and thus unprepared. According to William Ide, "Emigrants are generally too impatient, and over-drive their teams, and cattle...They often neglect the concerns of the present, in consequence of great anticipations of the future - they long to see what the next elevation hides from their view." Members of the Hudson's Bay Company working in Oregon Territory also commented on the lack of experience of many migrants, and that many travelers arrived "destitute both of clothing, even the necessarys of life, and are not in general what may be called enlightened Citizens, but in most cases, the scum and refuse of the back States... Many of them came across with wagons; how they managed to get thro or over the mountains with their clumsy machines, is the wonder and talk of this side of the mountains." While much of the negativity toward overland travelers stemmed from the fact that they viewed the Americans as a threat to their (British) claims to the Northwest, these British workers also accurately described the amateur nature of overland westward migration, and how many of those who undertook the journey west were Easterners completely unfamiliar with the geography and conditions that they would face along the Oregon Trail.

Missionaries also had a dim view of those traveling across the Oregon Trail. For George Gary, "It is not easy to calculate the depravity of many of the emigrants to this country." Francis Parkman added, "For the most part, they were the rudest and most ignorant of the frontier population; they knew absolutely nothing of the country and its inhabitants."

It's clear that those who wrote about the settlers of the 1830s concentrated on the sordid nature of the men, and it's almost certainly true that plenty of the people were heading to the West because they had burned their bridges back home, but many of the travelers moving west came as families. In fact, wagon companies were often made up of several families linked by blood or marriage, and during the 1850s and 1860s, women and children made up a substantial portion of the members of the wagon trains. At the same time, preparing families for the move west was a complicated endeavor, requiring the purchase of supplies, wagons, and livestock. The cost of overland travel has been estimated by historians at roughly $100 to $200 per person, which amounts to between $2,200 and $4,500 per person today. One veteran of the Oregon Trail, John Unruh, put the cost for a family at $1,500, or about $33,000 today. The challenges of preparing for the trip west was based on the fact that wagon trains would have virtually no help once they moved beyond Fort Leavenworth in present-day Kansas. Before the Mexican-American War, there were no American soldiers north of Texas, and the few forts manned by fur-trappers and Indian traders during this early period were not equipped to give any help to the wagon trains.

The first party to reach the Columbia River entirely by wagon arrived in 1843. This group was known as the "Great Migration," and it consisted of 900 people and 100 wagons, with as many as 700 head of cattle. In 1844, some 1,500 people made the journey, and the number grew to 2,500 in 1845. In 1847, that figure rose to 4,000. Between 1840 and 1860, an estimated 53,000 settlers traveled from various places along the Missouri River to the Oregon territory, settling mostly in the Willamette Valley.

To this movement of American settlers along the overland route from the east can be added those that made the journey by sea. This was a smaller number, but it still amounted to several thousand people. More still drifted north from California after the Gold Rush of 1849 had run its course, and yet others came from the north, usually French voyagers and traders. In 1844, Oregon City, located a few miles upstream of the present-day city of Portland, became the first incorporated municipality west of the Rocky Mountains, and by far the largest urban settlement in the territory. Portland soon superseded Oregon City, and within a decade, Seattle would be more prominent than both.

The Oregon Treaty

By the mid-1840s, it was clear the era of the palisade fort, trading post, and itinerate fur trader was over. Thousands of settlers were filling up the Willamette Valley and filtering out into the remote country east of the Cascades. Farms were demarcated, roads were established, and towns and settlements were incorporated.

Still, no formal government of any sort yet existed, and neither side seemed in any hurry to change that. Indeed, the attitude of both the British and U.S. governments to the question of Oregon remained at the very least ambivalent. In 1818, and again in 1827, Great Britain and the United States agreed only to joint occupation of the Oregon Country, deferring the question of a final division until some time in the future. The Oregon Country comprised a region stretching from the present Oregon-California border to "Fifty-four-Forty," a point just above the 54th Parallel, beyond which was Russian territory.

From the British point of view, the situation was more acceptable since British subjects were still few in number there and were, for the most part, subject to the rule of the Hudson's Bay

Company. Although imperfect, this arrangement was, at least for the time being, adequate for everyone involved. Law and order in the territory was generally attended to by the company, which was no major burden since the population was minimal.

Americans, on the other hand, lay not only outside the jurisdiction of the Hudson's Bay Company, but also beyond the practical reach of the laws of the United States. Congress appeared unconcerned by this, and despite repeated petitions to declare the region a U.S. "Territory," no steps in that direction were taken. The obvious reason for this was that the territory was jointly claimed, and no arbitrary solution could be imposed without lengthy negotiations with the British authorities. In fact, neither side showed much interest in attending to those negotiations, so things were left as they stood, even as it left the American population of the territory in limbo. The only alternative to American law was British law, and there certainly was no appetite south of the Columbia River for that. The debate within the American community was therefore simply whether to go ahead and form an independent government or to wait indefinitely for Congress to act.

It was inevitable that collective decision making and questions of law would require the formation of a committee or something similar, and that would, in turn, represent a style of government. The first such committee was formed over the question of probate for the intestate estate of a wealthy landowner. To dispose of his property, the assembled committee met on three separate occasions, and in effect the committee disposed of a legal process to the satisfaction of all. Settler representatives then met in March 1843 to discuss the question of wildlife attacks on livestock and how to form a common and coordinated response. Funds were collected and accumulated for the hiring of professional hunters, advancing somewhat the new parameters of self-government. The so-called "Wolf Meetings" established a basis of rudimentary taxation, along with a system of centralized contracting for a specific, collective social service.

A few months later, some 100 American and French Canadian settlers met at Champoeg, a settlement of the latter. The French Canadians, incidentally, were part of an early settlement of people employed by the Hudson's Bay Company, augmented over time by French and Belgian immigrants arriving in the area from Europe. They were not happy with either British or American law, although, since they were French, they were more disposed to the latter. In May 1843, by a slim majority, the motion was carried to form a provisional government. Most French speakers dissented, and John McLoughlin for the Hudson's Bay Company, although on cordial terms with all of the signatories and committee members, recorded his refusal to recognize the new government. In general, this decision heightened political tension between the British and Americans in the Pacific Northwest, but on a practical level, everyone involved, even McLoughlin, acknowledged that the process was inevitable and that some fundamental division of the territory was now imminent.

Using the resources at their disposal, which at the time comprised a single copy of the Organic

Laws of the State of Iowa, a copy of the U.S. Constitution, and one of the Declaration of Independence, a rudimentary system of laws was devised. These, and a patchwork of established traditions and simple statues, were combined into a constitution that established the basis and instruments of government. The new constitution provided for a single executive, compulsory taxation, a ban on alcoholic beverages, and the exclusion of blacks from the territory.

Whatever the British authorities in the territory might have felt about these events, there was little that they could do. Within the expanding United States, the concept of "Manifest Destiny" was fast gaining momentum as an expression of vast confidence and a growing sense of what was possible as Americans gazed across the vast and empty expanse of the continent with a sense that it was theirs. In the face of that, British mercantile interests above the Columbia River presented a weak bulwark. The eventual annexation of Texas and the occupation of Oregon were the battle cries of this movement, and to them, taking Oregon implied the entirety of the territory from the border of California to the mythical "Fifty-four-Forty." In fact, American expansionists took up a much more belligerent battle cry, proclaiming "Fifty-four-Forty or Fight!"

Nonetheless, opinion was divided in Congress. While the popular mood throughout the country was bullish and aggressive, within Congress, there were those who did not necessarily acknowledge the value of the territory, other than perhaps as a penal colony. Occasional meetings of British and American plenipotentiaries were held over the matter, but neither side seemed interested in pursuing the matter further than that.

It was not until the inauguration of President James K. Polk in March 1845 that the matter was elevated higher up the list of government priorities. In his inaugural speech, Polk remarked that the American claim to Oregon was "clear and unquestionable." After that, it was Polk who took the matter up, proposing to the British that the territory be divided along the 49th Parallel. When the British declined, Polk took a more assertive position, declaring that American honor and interests were at stake and that he was unprepared to compromise.

Polk

There very few outside of the extremist fringe who believed that the United States had any defensible claim to the entire Oregon Country. In the Willamette Valley and other pockets of land south of the Columbia River, citizens of the United States certainly predominated, but above the line of the Columbia River, although the non-native population remained minimal, it was nonetheless predominately British. Above the 49th Parallel, there were no Americans at all. The focus of the dispute, then, was the territory to the north and west of the Columbia River, which comprised the modern state of Washington.

There were many reasons for the unyielding American position in this regard, but trade and commerce remained the strongest incentives. There was a lack of practical harbors north of San Francisco, which remained for the time being Spanish, and the only region of viable harbors between the 42nd Parallel and the 49th Parallel was Puget Sound. Thus, in order for the United States to secure an economic position on the Pacific coast and have access to Asian markets, it was essential to secure the possession of this stretch of the coast.

The timing was also fortuitous because the British had other problems elsewhere. A series of frontier wars in the colony of New Zealand had broken out, and British political and military resources tended to be focused there. The potato blight took place in Ireland, triggering the Great Famine that would see hundreds of thousands of impoverished Irish come to America. Then, in India, the first of the Sikh Wars erupted, further concentrating British attention east. It was in 1846 too that President Polk announced the Monroe Doctrine was to be rigidly enforced, and that the United States should aggressively move west.

Nonetheless, the political system did not always respond with the same enthusiasm as some of its leaders. Congressional debate on the matter dragged on until the spring of 1846 when the United States once again invited Great Britain to the negotiating table. In May of that year, Polk completed the annexation of Texas, regarded often as the first overt act of American imperialism, which, if nothing else, confirmed that this time Congress was serious. In April, the Mexican-American War began, and it would end in the 1848 annexation of California. America was on the march, and Manifest Destiny was manifest indeed.

By then, the Hudson's Bay Company had moved its operational headquarters to Victoria Island in the future British Columbia, and the Columbia region was of less direct importance to its operations. Besides that, the British were still preoccupied with fighting in India, uprisings in New Zealand, starving Irishmen, and a political crisis at home, the latter of which would see Conservative Prime Minister Robert Peel yield power to the Whig Lord John Russell. Put simply, the business of a boundary in the remote Pacific Northwest was not of particular interest, and to Polk's surprise, an agreement was relatively easily reached. The 49th Parallel was accepted as the new international boundary, with a slight manipulation in the area of Vancouver Island to ensure that it was British territory. There was some grumbling about this in Washington, but it was accepted as inevitable. The Hudson's Bay Company retained the right to freely navigate the Columbia River south of the 49th Parallel until 1860.

The treaty was ratified by the Senate in June 1846, but for a while after that, a rather poorly defined water boundary south of Vancouver Island caused some jostling and acrimony which was brought a head by the curious episode of the "Pig War" of 1859. The events of this minor scuffle are, if nothing else, a reminder of how easily wars can be started. The area contested was the San Juan Islands, a small archipelago clustered at the southeastern heel of Vancouver Island. The islands were claimed by both sides, and a cold war of sorts existed, with neither side willing to back down. One day, a British-owned pig strayed onto an American-owned potato patch and was killed, triggering a dispute between citizens on both sides. It was then backed up by a military display and some posturing on both sides that stopped just short of shots being fired. It was agreed that the islands would remain under joint military administration until 1872, when the dispute was arbitrated in favor of the United States by Kaiser Wilhelm I, the newly coronated emperor of Germany. The British were heard to complain in the aftermath that no German monarch was likely ever to rule in favor of Great Britain, but nonetheless, the San Juan Islands passed to the United States, and that seemed to be the end of the matter.

Statehood

The formal settlement of the longstanding boundary dispute did not immediately answer the remaining questions of governance, and little on the ground truly changed in terms of daily life. That all changed, however, in the wake of the Whitman Massacre, which instigated a period of violence and insecurity on the western frontier of the territory. Known as the Cayuse Wars, it resulted in the banishment of the native peoples of the region to reservations, and it galvanized the federal government to act over the status of the Oregon Country.

In May 1848, the former mountain man Joseph Meek arrived in St. Louis after an overland journey from Oregon in the dead of winter, announcing himself as the "Envoy Extraordinary and Minister Plenipotentiary from the Republic of Oregon to the Court of the United States." In fact, Joseph Meek was a representative of the provisional government sent to plead for the establishment of U.S. "Territory" status for Oregon. The essential message that he carried on behalf of the provisional government was that if the United States had attended to its duties earlier, the Whitman Massacre and subsequent violence might never have happened.

The Oregon Territory was formally created as an Act of Congress in August of that year, with Meek appointed marshal and Joseph Lane of Indiana, a hero of the Mexican-American War, named its first governor. Lane arrived in the Territory on March 2, 1849, and the next day he formally declared the existence of the Oregon Territory. Several weeks later, the U.S. Army established bases alongside Fort Vancouver and Fort Nisqually, and soon after that, mail service began running.

Lane

Meek

Despite becoming a U.S. Territory, Oregon suffered from certain limitations. A "Territory," as defined by the Constitution, is a region belonging to the United States, but not within the boundaries of any existing state. According to Article IV of the Constitution, "The Congress shall have Power to dispose of and make all needful Rules and Regulations respecting the Territory or other Property belonging to the United States; and nothing in this Constitution shall be so construed as to Prejudice any Claims of the United States, or of any particular State."

In other words, even though the governor and administration were appointed, Congress retained sweeping powers. It was empowered, for example, to set the limits of legislative sessions, determine the number of legislators, and veto any enactments. Congress could also set territorial boundaries, which accounts for the existence and unique shape of Idaho. However, in practical terms, while the federal government met the cost of most territorial expenses, it hardly involved itself at all in administrative affairs. Federal power resided with the governor, supported by a secretary, three or more justices, and any subordinate federal officials required to dispose of federal business in the Territory. Each Territory was entitled to select a representative for Congress, but that representative typically lacked a vote or any other formal power enjoyed by elected members of Congress. Territorial representatives, therefore, functioned primarily as lobbyists, publicists, and dispensers of federal aid and political favors in the territories. Joseph Lane was elected several times as that representative, thereby emerging as a powerful political figure both in Oregon and in national Democratic circles.

The political debate within the Oregon Territory involved the fundamentals of identity and structure. It took a great deal of acrimonious debate, therefore, before the location of the territorial capital could be fixed at Salem, and even more to determine where Oregon stood in the great slavery debate of the time.

The slavery debate in the Pacific Northwest played out over almost two decades, growing more bitter and acrimonious as more and more settlers from the committed slave states arrived and brought slaves with them. On a purely practical level, the Willamette Valley, the agricultural heartland of the Territory, was ideal for large-scale production, and with a mild climate, it was also ideal for slave labor. Under the "Organic Laws of Oregon," drafted during the Champoeg Meetings, slavery was illegal, yet a handful of Oregonians owned slaves. There were also numerous advocates of slavery, of course, in particular among Democrats. They included Governor Lane himself.

In 1857, the Supreme Court of the United States issued a landmark ruling in the *Dred Scott* case, which in essence prevented black people whose ancestors were imported as slaves from ever being regarded as a citizen. As such, blacks could not file suit in a federal court. The case centered around the efforts of a black slave, Dred Scott, to sue for his freedom after his removal to a non-slave state. A corollary of this judgement was to disallow territorial, but not state law in regards to slavery, which some historians have cited as a reason why a general movement towards statehood began to gather momentum in the aftermath of this ruling. Thus, the Oregon Constitution of 1857, approved by Congress only after lengthy debate, came into effect in 1859. In the end, the Oregon Constitution declared its opposition to slavery, even as it also excluded blacks from the land entirely, becoming the only American state to do so by means other than ordinary statutory law.

With that, on February 14, 1859, after being a U.S. Territory for about a decade, Oregon became the 33rd state.

By then, however, the vast Oregon Territory, comprising an area of some 350,000 square miles, diverse in cultural aspects and unmanageable as a single geographic and political unit, had already been divided. The main population concentrations ran along the Willamette Valley, where the state capital of Salem was located. Widespread and diverse populations were scattered in the arid east where the border of the state was only vaguely defined. To the north, however, above the Columbia River, known informally as Northern Oregon, the population was also sparse, but growing steadily. There was, quite naturally, a sense in the north that state affairs were dominated by the south, especially the powerful lobbies of the Willamette Valley and the growing metropolises of Portland and Salem.

It could certainly not be denied that resources across the two regions were unevenly balanced, and by the date of statehood, only some 4,000 whites resided between the Columbia River and the 49th Parallel. Settlers in that region were quick to organize as the Oregon Territory moved towards statehood, holding two general settler meetings, the first in Cowlitz Prairie in August 1851 and the second in Monticello, or modern-day Longview, in September 1852. The objective of the meetings was to form a consensus on submitting a request to Congress for the establishment of a separate territory north of the Columbia River. No particular representation to the contrary was heard from south of the Columbia River, so on May 2, 1853, legislation was approved by Congress creating a new territory named after the nation's first president.

The first governor of the Washington Territory was Isaac I. Stevens, a native of Massachusetts and an ex-officer of the Engineering Corps during the Mexican-American War. Characterized by a mild form of dwarfism, Stevens seemed driven by passionate energy to succeed despite what was at the time more of a social disability than a physical one. A star graduate of West Point, his military service was exemplary, and as governor of the Washington Territory, he served also in the roles of Indian Agent and head of a national railway survey, which he championed as part of a drive to attract immigrants and settlers.

Stevens

If Isaac Stevens is remembered for anything in Washington, it is perhaps his heavy-handed settlement of a number of outstanding Indian land issues with the tribes of Washington, western Idaho, and Montana. Stevens wanted settlers, settlers needed land, and treaty negotiations to get that land were both forceful and perfunctory. As such, when the complexity of these negotiations defeated the basics of interpretation, Stevens simply appointed "chiefs" and "sub-chiefs" to sign on behalf of the various native landholders. It was neither an admirable nor honest process, and in general, Stevens' attitude to the 17,000 or so native residents in Washington was paternalistic, at least when it was not entirely indifferent. In the end, title to more than 64 million acres of land was acquired in this way, in exchange for nothing more than retention of fishing rights, various federal allowances and annuities, and the supply of tools, equipment, and training for agriculture.

Even in Washington, this process was regarded with deep circumspection. Congress sat on the matter and did not ratify many of these treaties for a considerable time. They were nonetheless acted upon and became in effect a fait accompli. It was all done in unseemly haste, and once the signatories were given the opportunity to reflect on the details of the transfers, a great deal of discontent was expressed, and there were occasional outbreaks of violence. Likewise, whites did not always acknowledge and respect the land and fishing rights, and disputes in that quarter were also frequent.

Stevens then won election as Washington's representative to Congress, joining his friend and fellow delegate Joseph Lane as a key member of the Democratic Party.

Meanwhile, the same unmanageable mass of territory that burdened the early administration of Oregon also began to challenge the Washington Territory. When Oregon was granted statehood and Washington was separated from it, it meant that a vast, but sparsely settled region stretching from the Olympic Peninsula to the Rocky Mountains, incorporating Idaho and large sections of western Montana and Wyoming, came under the administration of the Washington Territory. The capital of Washington was established at Olympia, on the southern shores of the Puget Sound, and the vast distances between it and the far-flung outposts of the Territory rendered effective administration virtually impossible.

In 1860, a minor gold rush was sparked in the region of the Clearwater River of central Idaho when gold was discovered on Nez Percé land by Elias Davidson Pierce, a native of Harris County, West Virginia. Pierce City was established, and within a year it numbered 4,000 residents. By the summer of 1863, some 35,000 whites were settled in the interior regions. The isolated frontier settlement of Walla Walla emerged as a significant link in the supply chain of goods and equipment into the interior, and for a while, there were fears in Olympia that it might take over as the administrative capital of the territory. The subsequent discovery of gold in Montana added a further complication to the conundrum of controlling and governing an ever-expanding territory.

There was very little regret felt in Olympia, therefore, when, on March 4, 1863, Congress made the decision to combine Washington's far-flung mining regions into a new territory called Idaho. The former governor of the Washington Territory, William H. Wallace, was appointed by President Abraham Lincoln as the first territorial governor of Idaho.

Idaho has always been regarded in the historical development of states as an ill-conceived anomaly, with its territorial boundaries at one time encompassing all of Montana and most of Wyoming. Even after Idaho's boundaries receded in 1864 and again in 1868, the territory remained economically and culturally divided. To travel by train from the panhandle to Boise required leaving the territory and changing trains in Spokane. No paved highway linked the north and south of the state until 1937, and even by the turn of the century, it was still quicker to travel from the panhandle to Olympia or Helena, Montana than it was to Boise.

Idaho's status as a U.S. Territory lasted for 27 years, during which it was constantly on the brink of insolvency. In his *Interpretive History of the Pacific Northwest*, Dr. Carlos A.

Schwantes remarked of the succession of territorial governors, "Governors were for the most part an odd lot of scheming or incompetent carpetbag politicians who seemed to serve the territory best by leaving it – or not arriving at all."

Washington was granted statehood on November 11, 1889, as the 42nd state. Idaho followed months later as the 43rd.

Of course, even as American politicians were trying to sort out the political issues and boundaries, there were still plenty of natives living on the land being claimed. In 1861, the Washington legislature passed an ordinance forbidding marriage between whites and Indians, criminalizing a practice that had been ongoing for decades. The interracial nature of the early days of mercantile settlements were generally the days of peace and harmony, but after the Whitman Massacre, nothing was ever the same again. The decade before it had never been free of violence, but Indians were so integral to the fur trade that usually petty differences were settled in one way or another to the satisfaction of both sides.

The years of the fur trade were not years of mass European settlement, and certainly not years of mass land appropriation. The dispossession of the native people of the region was a result of America's push west, and the Whitman Massacre coincided with that transition and the efforts of indigenous people to resist the monumental changes that white settlement caused, few of which were to their advantage. A contributing factor, of course, was the fundamental failure of each side to appreciate or understand the other, a phenomenon repeated in India, Africa, and other places that imperialistic powers came into contact with older, indigenous populations.

In many respects, the indigenous people of the Pacific Northwest suffered the same fate as Australian Aborigines. They were not resilient to alcohol and had no immunity against European diseases, so their numbers diminished steadily as whites advanced. They were also not perceived as a viable source of labor, so their occupation of the land was nothing more than an inconvenience.

In that regard, the Whitman Massacre served the useful purposes of demonizing the native people and planting a seed of distrust and bitterness that rendered possible much of what would subsequently take place. Between 1851 and 1868, most of the natives of Oregon were relocated onto reservation land, and indeed, the first superintendent of Indian Affairs, Anson Dart, pushed for the removal of all Indians across the cascades and onto reserves in the arid regions to the east. Native cultures evolved in the lush countryside of the coast, and Willamette Valley could hardly so quickly adapt, so the effort was bitterly resisted and never acted upon. It was indicative of the pressures and the attitudes of the time.

The first serious trouble erupted in the Rouge River Country, close to the California border, as prospectors, miners, and homesteaders began to filter into the region, pressing up against a confederation known as the Rouge River Indians. The first bout of violence was brought to an end by the Table Rock Treaty of 1853.

The Table Rock Treaty established a temporary reservation, which, in fact, was the first of its kind in the Pacific Northwest, known as the "Table Rock Indian Reservation." The treaty also provided for a military fort, Fort Lane, ostensibly to protect Indian interests. The Table Rock Treaty was hailed in many quarters as a landmark, and it became the template for numerous others to replicate. Tensions, however, continued to mount between incoming whites and nervous natives, erupting into a full-scale war in 1855.

Also, in 1855, war broke out further north in the Washington Territory. Isaac Stevens, acting with typical haste and little reflection, sought to hurry along a solution by concentrating all of the Indians of his territory on reservation land while opening up the remainder of the territory to white settlement. According to Doctor Carlos A. Schwantes, "Quite simply, the Governor and many others never questioned the necessity of removing Indians from the path of white civilization, although he did hope that it could be accomplished peacefully and through negotiations."

Stevens' style of negotiation was simply to bully and harangue, and one treaty negotiation after another pushed the native population into dispersed and inadequate reservations. In general, he found it easier to allocate small areas of traditional land, replacing semi-nomadic lifestyles with settled ones based on traditional hunting and fishing rights and instruction in farming techniques. Any resistance was met by force, and in the end, Stevens gained 45,000 square miles of land in exchange for three reservations and vague promises for more.

The fragility of it all was revealed when gold was discovered along the Columbia River in 1855, bringing hordes of gold-seekers onto the recently demarcated Yakima reservation in absolute disregard of the terms of the treaty. The natives rose in violent protest, in response to which Stevens declared martial law and the Yakima were violently subdued.

To the east of the Cascades, war broke out in 1858 as the tribes of the Columbia Basin (except the Nez Percé) combined to resist ongoing white encroachment. A combined force of Spokanes, Yakimas, Coeur d'Alenes and Palooses inflicted a rare defeat on the US Army. This might have briefly raised spirits, but the inevitable response was simply greater force, and what was known as the "Yakima War" was brought to an end with the significant loss of life and property.

That was the last episode in Washington, while in Oregon, violence tended to be restricted to minor incidents involving small groups or individuals, and that remained the case until the outbreak of what came to be known as the Modoc War along the California-Oregon border in 1873. The cause of this conflict was no different, but this time, in a remote region, well-organized resistance kept the U.S. Army at bay, claiming 120 U.S. Army casualties. This was not the kind of setback the U.S. Army typically experienced when fighting Native Americans, and things only got worse when General Edward Canby, a decorated Civil War hero, was shot and killed under a flag of truce. The conflict lasted six months and ended with the hanging of the principal Modoc leaders and the exile of 155 prisoners to reservations in Oklahoma.

Some of the most sustained and brutal fighting of the conflict took place in Idaho, and at the Battle of Bear River in 1863, between 200 and 400 mostly Shoshones were killed. Perhaps the most documented incident of the period was the Nez Percé War of 1877. The Nez Percé were subject to one of Stevens' treaty filibusters. However, shrinking reservations and white encroachments caused "non-treaty" groups to occupy land outside the reservation. This was indulged by local and federal authorities until the land began to fill up with whites, and the Nez Percé were inevitably pressured to return to the reservations. Four settlers were killed by a rogue group of young Nez Percé, and war followed soon afterwards.

During mid-1877, 800 Nez Percé men, women and children, along with a herd of more than 2,000 horses, took flight across the Bitterroot Mountains, where they hoped to find sanctuary among the Crow, or alternatively to find asylum in Canada. They were pursued by a detachment of the U.S. Army, led by the one-armed Colonel Oliver Otis Howard. On August 9-10, the defining Battle of the Big Hole was fought, ending inevitably in a defeat for the Nez Percé band. The flight continued, however, growing ever more desperate with each mile. The refugees crossed the Montana territory through the Yellowstone National Park, continuing on to the 49th Parallel. Just 40 miles south of that goal, they were intercepted. After a 1,700-mile exodus, only 480 Nez Percé were present to surrender. The captives were exiled to Oklahoma and permitted to return to the Northwest only in 1885.

By 1880, most natives were settled on reservations. Ostensibly, it had been achieved by treaties and negotiations, but in reality, it was a combination of diseases, exhaustion, diminishing numbers, and the pressure of white expansion that solved the land disputes in the Oregon Country and allowed for permanent boundaries to be established in the Pacific Northwest.

Online Resources

Other books about 19th century American history by Charles River Editors

Other books about Oregon on Amazon

Further Reading

Bagley, Will. So Rugged and Mountainous: Blazing the Trails to Oregon and California, 1812-1848. Norman, OK: University of Oklahoma Press, 2010.

Faragher, John Mack. Women and Men on the Overland Trail (2nd ed. 2001) excerpt and text search

Federal Writers' Project. The Oregon trail: the Missouri river to the Pacific ocean (1939) online edition, 244pp

Hanson, T J (2001). Western Passage. Bookmasters, Inc. ISBN 0-9705847-0-9.

Holmes, Kenneth L. Covered Wagon Women: Diaries and Letters from the Western Trails. Lincoln: University of Nebraska Press, 1991.

Morgan, Dale Lowell. Overland in 1846: Diaries and Letters of the California-Oregon Trail. Georgetown, CA: Talisman Press, 1963.

Unruh, John David. The Plains Across: The Overland Emigrants and the Trans-Mississippi West, 1840–1860 (1993) University of Illinois Press. ISBN 978-0-252-06360-2, the standard scholarly history

Free Books by Charles River Editors

We have brand new titles available for free most days of the week. To see which of our titles are currently free, click on this link.

Discounted Books by Charles River Editors

We have titles at a discount price of just 99 cents everyday. To see which of our titles are currently 99 cents, [click on this link](.).

Printed in Great Britain
by Amazon